WHERE DID IT COME FROM?

INVENTING SCISSORS

by Emma Carlson Berne

Consultant: Beth Gambro
Reading Specialist, Yorkville, Illinois

BEARPORT PUBLISHING

Bearcub Books, an imprint of Bearport Publishing by FlutterBee

Teaching Tips

Before Reading

- Look at the cover of the book. Discuss the picture and the title.
- Ask readers to brainstorm a list of what they already know about scissors. What can they expect to see in the book?
- Go on a picture walk, looking through the pictures to discuss vocabulary and make predictions about the text.

During Reading

- Read for purpose. Encourage readers to think about the inspiration behind making scissors as they are reading.
- Ask readers to look for the details of the book. What were some of the first uses for scissors?
- If readers encounter an unknown word, ask them to look at the sounds in the word. Then, ask them to look at the rest of the page. Are there any clues to help them understand?

After Reading

- Encourage readers to pick a buddy and reread the book together.
- Ask readers to name two things that happened as scissors were being invented. Find the pages that tell about these things.
- Ask readers to write or draw something they learned about scissors.

Credits
Cover and title page, © vi mart/Shutterstock and © Veja/Shutterstock; 3, © Oleksandr Kostiuchenko/Shutterstock; 5, © Yuriy Golub/Shutterstock; 7, © Morphart Creation/Shutterstock; 9, © Andrea Izzotti/Alamy Stock Photo; 11, © vectorlight/Shutterstock and © durmus1986/Shutterstock; 13, © LMA/AW/Alamy Stock Photo; 15, © Lebrecht Music && Arts/Alamy Stock Photo; 17, © Vladi333/Getty Images; 19, © Elegant01/Alamy Stock Photo; 21, © LightField Studios/Shutterstock; 22T, © vitranc/iStock; 22M, © PAKAPORN YAMANON/iStock; 22B, © Dan Thornberg/Shutterstock; 23TL, © PrimeMockup/Shutterstock; 23TR, © andresr/iStock; 23BL, © Urri/Shutterstock; 23BR, © Sevaljevic/iStock.

See BearportPublishing.com for our statement on Generative AI Usage.

Library of Congress Cataloging-in-Publication Data is available at www.loc.gov or upon request from the publisher.

ISBN: 979-8-89577-589-9 (hardcover)
ISBN: 979-8-89577-769-5 (paperback)
ISBN: 979-8-89577-677-3 (ebook)

For more information, write to Bearport Publishing, 3500 American Blvd W, Suite 150, Bloomington, MN 55431.
Printed in the United States of America.

Contents

Snip! 4

Fun Scissors Facts 22

Glossary 23

Index 24

Read More 24

Learn More Online 24

About the Author 24

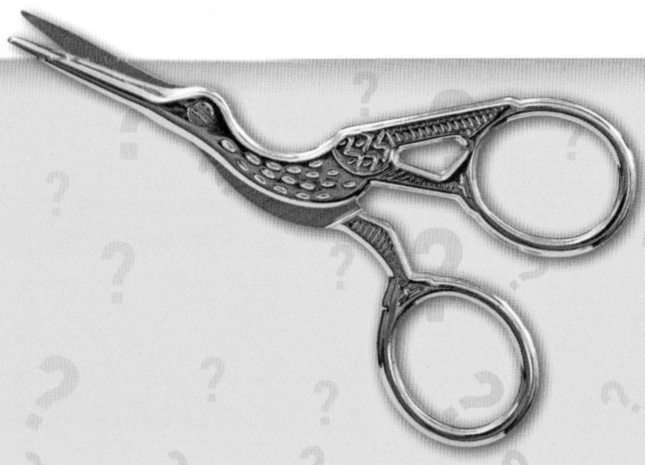

Snip!

Scissors cut through paper.

They snip hair and cloth.

There are so many uses for scissors.

But where did scissors come from?

For a long time, people have used **blades** to cut things.

They trimmed fur off animals to make clothes.

This was called **shearing**.

But cutting with blades took a long time.

People needed something easier.

So, they made scissors.

The first scissors were made 3,000 years ago.

They came from Mesopotamia.

Say Mesopotamia like *me*-suh-puh-TAY-mee-uh

NORTH AMERICA
SOUTH AMERICA
EUROPE
ASIA
AFRICA
AUSTRALIA
Mesopotamia

These tools had two blades.

The blades came together when the scissors were squeezed.

They sprung open when the scissors were let go.

People made these scissors from **bronze**.

This metal could be sharpened easily.

It could also bend when squeezed.

With this tool, people could cut much quicker.

And they could cut things more carefully.

Scissors spread all around the world.

Later, people in Rome and China made new scissors.

These had two pieces **connected** in the middle.

Now, we use scissors for so many things.

They help us with our work and when we make art.

Snip, snip!

Let's get cutting!

Fun Scissors Facts

Some scissors are so sharp they can cut through metal.

One of the pairs of scissors that costs the most is used to trim plants.

The world's largest pair of scissors is as long as a small canoe!

Glossary

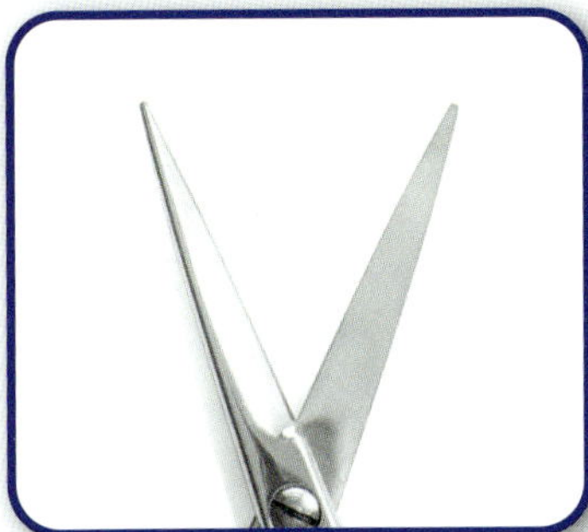

blades sharp tools used for cutting

bronze a metal made from copper and tin

connected joined or linked together

shearing cutting or clipping something

Index

blades 6, 8, 12
China 18
hair 4
Mesopotamia 10–11
paper 4
Rome 18

Read More

Mather, Charis. *Haircuts (Level 4–Blue Set).* Minneapolis: Jump! 2024.

Winters, C.E. *Cut! How Lotte Reiniger and a Pair of Scissors Revolutionized Animation.* New York: HarperCollins, 2023.

Learn More Online

1. Go to **FactSurfer.com** or scan the QR code below.
2. Enter "**Inventing Scissors**" into the search box.
3. Click on the cover of this book to see a list of websites.

About the Author

Emma Carlson Berne is the author of many books. She lives in Cincinnati, Ohio, with her husband, three children, one grumpy cat, and one friendly cat.